"Hello."

I'm Caitlin.
I love making
music and
singing.

What do you like doing best?

I especially like it when Mum and Dad play their drums with me. It can get very noisy!

What do you like doing with your family?

We all sing before our meals to show we are thankful for our food. My favourite food is chocolate but Dad says I have to eat vegetables too!

Who do you thank for your food?

My dad is a very good cook – especially when we have a barbecue in the summer!

What is your favourite food?

When I go to school, I love learning new things from my teacher and my friends.

Who helps you learn new things?

At home I like learning about Prince Siddhartha and how he became wise and called Buddha.

Do you have a favourite story about a special person?

One night, about 2,500 years ago, under a bright moon and shining stars, Queen Maya gave birth to a little boy. The king and queen called their baby Prince Siddhartha Gautama.

The prince was a happy boy, living in a beautiful palace
and surrounded by everything he could wish for. He loved
all the animals and birds that lived in the palace grounds.

When Siddhartha grew up and left the palace, he realised that other people's lives are not always so happy. Often people feel sad and troubled and he wanted to help them find happiness.

One day, after sitting for a very long time, Siddhartha realised he knew how to help others find happiness and peace. People called him the Buddha. From that day on, the Buddha shared his wise teachings to help people find happiness.

My family are Buddhists. We try to follow the Buddha's teachings. We try to be happy and wise.

What rules or teachings do you try to follow?

The Buddha taught that we should always be kind to one another and all living creatures.

How do you show care for all living creatures?

Mum and Dad say that if we feel happy in ourselves it's easier to be kind to others.

How do you show kindness?

My mum and dad sometimes wear special clothes to show they are Buddhist teachers.

Do you know of any special clothes that are worn to show what people belong to or believe?

Mum and Dad try to help other people become happy and wise. They like to answer people's questions about the Buddha.

At our Buddhist Centre the adults often do yoga to help them feel happy and peaceful. I think it looks really hard to do!

Meditating also helps people to be happy and peaceful. They try to become wise just like a Buddha.

Sometimes we make beautiful namkhas. When we weave the wool, we think about our different feelings.

When do feel happy, sad, angry, peaceful, worried, safe?

Cutting and sticking and making things with my mum, always makes me feel happy.

Our shrine room is a special place where I feel peaceful. We always take off our shoes before we go in to keep it clean and show our respect.

Do you have a special place where you think about someone or something important?

The special things in our shrine room help us think about teachings from the Buddhas.

What things are special to you?

One day I would like to visit other countries to see the many different images of Buddhas all over the world.

Teachers' / parents'/ carers' notes relating to specific pages

Buddhism
In the notes below, we have used the term "Buddhists" in the generic sense only. In order to take account of the variety of expressions of faith, it is always advisable to modify speech by using terms such as "many Buddhists", "some Buddhists" or "Buddhists often".

1, 2 – Religious Tradition
Caitlin and her family follow the Tibetan Vajrayana Buddhist tradition and in particular the Aro gTér lineage. Within their lineage, music (both singing and instrumental) can be used as a meditation technique in itself and also to complement silent sitting meditation. Caitlin particularly likes playing Himalayan musical instruments such as the drilbu (bell), chod drum, dungchen (great horn), conch, and the silnyen and rolmo (peaceful and wrathful cymbals).

3, 4 – Diet
The family have a special song they sing before their meals to show their appreciation for food. It is sung in Tibetan and is a story about Padmasambhava's life and teaching (see page 14, 15 notes). It is sung in order to remember all the living beings – people, plants and animals – who are connected with enabling the meal to happen.

Buddhism has no specific teachings regarding diet. Whilst some Buddhists may choose a vegetarian diet, this is a personal choice. The Buddha taught that one should not wilfully harm any living creature (ahimsa) and that it is for each individual to determine how they interpret that teaching within their daily lives.

5 – Education and Views on Other Beliefs
Caitlin attends her local village Church in Wales school. She is happy to learn about the Christian faith and other religions and worldviews in religous education lessons as part of the school curriculum.

As Buddhists, Caitlin's family respects the right of others to uphold different beliefs and practices in relation to faith and non-religious views. Buddhism promotes respect for other people's beliefs, teachings and practices. The Buddha did not want people to follow his teachings blindly but to test them for themselves. From the Buddhist point of view, a wide choice of religions is needed to suit the varied needs of different people. Buddhists can encourage others to practise their own religions, provided that they promote the well-being of all living beings.

6 – Founder
Buddhism started with the birth of Prince Siddhartha Gautama who became the Buddha Shakyamuni.

It is reported that Prince Siddhartha Gautama was born into a royal family in the village of Lumbini in present-day Nepal around 563BCE.

He grew up as a Hindu which was the religion of the region at that time. He led a privileged life of luxury and his parents sheltered him from the outside world and an awareness of its usual sufferings of sickness, age and death.

After growing up, marrying and having a child, without ever having left the royal enclosure, he one day went outside the palace grounds and for the first time in his life saw an old man, a sick man, and a corpse. At that moment he learned that these conditions were an inevitable part of human life. Siddhartha also saw a holy man and decided this was the life he should live in order to seek a solution to the suffering he had witnessed. Siddhartha practised meditation and lived an extreme life of asceticism for six years but found that this did not give him the answers that he sought.

Having given up this extreme state of poverty, one day whilst sitting under a Bodhi tree Siddhartha became deeply absorbed in meditation, and finally achieved enlightenment and became known as the first or first of many Buddhas of this age.

He realised that living in the middle way between luxury and poverty was necessary in order to find a peaceful state of mind.

For the next 45 years of his life the Buddha taught many disciples, who became Arahants or 'noble ones', who attained Enlightenment for themselves. He passed away at the age of 80.

Sacred Texts
Buddhist teachings were initially passed on orally by monks, but approximately two hundred years after the Buddha's death, Emperor Asoka of India arranged for the teachings to be written down. The basic collection of writings is known as the Pali Canon and also as the Tripitaka as it is written in three parts:
- Vinaya - guidance for monks;
- Sutta – the Buddha's teachings; and
- Abhidhamma – higher teachings for intellectual academics.

Both Theravadin and Mahayanist Buddhists accept the Pali Canon as their sacred writings but Mahayanists also have many more authoritative texts such as the Sutras. Caitlin's family are from a section of Mahayana Buddhism called Vajrayana. It is particularly found in Tibet, Bhutan and Nepal and their texts are called Tantras.

Basic Beliefs
Buddhism is about practice rather than blind belief. Buddhists try to live in the "middle way", a path between the extremes of self-indulgence and self-denial. There are three 'Universal Truths' for Buddhists:
- Anicca – that everything is impermanent and subject to change;
- Dukkha – people's typical experience of life includes suffering or un-satisfactoriness; and
- Anatta – there is no soul but rather all beings are a series of mental and physical states.

Buddhists believe that Dukkha happens due to people creating negative patterns in their lives. These are called karmic patterns of perception and response. Karmic patterns could be likened to bad habits – like scratching an itch so much that it becomes sore. Samsara is the state of repeating negative patterns over and over again. Buddhists use meditation to change their perception and to open up and see the world as it really is. Meditation practice helps break bad habits and leads to Nirvana, a state of perfection.

11, 12, 13 – Key Teachings

The Buddhist way of life is one of peace, loving kindness and wisdom. The Buddha Shakyamuni taught that all problems and suffering arise from confused and negative states of mind, and that all happiness and good fortune arise from peaceful and positive states of mind.

The Buddha taught methods for gradually overcoming negative minds such as anger, jealousy and ignorance, and developing positive minds such as love, compassion and wisdom. Through this practice Buddhists aim to experience lasting wisdom and compassion. With wisdom and compassion, kindness naturally arises and with it, feelings of happiness, peacefulness and contentment.

The two main teachings are

The Four Noble Truths:
1 All life includes physical, emotional, mental suffering.
2 Suffering is due to selfish desire for that which is unattainable.
3 Suffering will cease if desire is ceased.
4 The way to cease desire is to follow the Noble Eightfold Path.

The Noble Eightfold Path (symbolised by a wheel):
1 Right View.
2 Right Thought.
3 Right Speech.
4 Right Action.
5 Right Livelihood/ Occupation.
6 Right Effort.
7 Right Mindfulness.
8 Right Concentration.

Buddhists aim to live by the Five Moral Precepts which are refraining from:
- harming living things;
- taking what is not given;
- sexual misconduct;
- lying or gossiping; and
- taking intoxicating substances such as drugs or alcohol.

Signs and Symbols

The main symbol associated with Buddhism is the wheel. Its eight spokes remind Buddhists that every part of the Noble Eightfold Path needs to be in place simultaneously for the 'wheel' to be in working order. The lotus flower is another important symbol (see page 19 plus corresponding notes).

12 – Views on the Natural World

The qualities of wisdom and compassion are considered the greatest qualities demonstrated by the Buddha. The Buddhist teaching of ahimsa – not to harm any living creature – means that compassion is shown to all animals, plants, and the world in general.

Buddhist do not have an account or story about creation. They believe in compassion for all sentient beings. Prince Siddhartha showed a concern for all living things as recalled in the story of him as a child, saving a swan. The Noble Eightfold Path includes a teaching of right livelihood which is taking an occupation that does no harm to any living being and to live in harmony with nature.

14, 15 – Teachers

All Buddhists trace their beliefs back to Buddha Shakyamuni. For Tibetan Vajrayana Buddhists, Padmasambhava is another important teacher who is also fully enlightened and therefore also known as a Buddha. It is said that Padmasambhava was born enlightened and some believe he is a reincarnation of Shakyamuni Buddha.

In Tibetan, the term Lama is used for teacher. For many Tibetan Buddhists the Dalai Lama is regarded as a very important teacher whilst some Tibetan and other Buddhist traditions acknowledge the importance of other spiritual leaders.

In Theravadin Buddhism, ordained teachers are mostly monastic monks (bhikkhus) or nuns (bhikkhunis).

In the Vajrayana tradition, followers can become ordained and remain living ordinary household lives. Caitlin's mum, Ngakma Shé-zér Khandro and dad, Ngakpa Namgyal Dorje are ordained and are teachers of the Aro gTér lineage. Ngakma and Ngakpa literally mean Mantrini or Mantrin – 'someone who recites mantra'. Their white robes and long hair are external symbols of their vows, just like red robes and shaven heads are symbols of Sutric monastic vows.

16 – Yoga

Yoga is a physical exercise which also focuses on the use of the breath and the well-being of the mind. It complements and supports silent sitting meditation practice and is therefore often taken up by Buddhists. The photograph shows a Tibetan Buddhist form of yoga called sKu-mNye (pronounced 'Koom-nyé').

17 – Meditation

Meditation is at the heart of the Buddhist way of life. It is essentially a method for understanding and working on the mind, firstly to learn to identify different negative mental states known as 'delusions', and then to learn how to develop peaceful and positive mental states or 'virtuous minds'.

As the state of mind becomes more positive, actions become

more constructive, and experience of life becomes more satisfying and beneficial to others.

Out of meditation Buddhists try to use the wisdom developed to solve the problems of daily life.

18 – Namkhas

Sky Weaving to create a namkha is an ancient Tibetan meditation practice. Namkha in Tibetan, means 'sky' or 'dimension'. This practice involves weaving 'skies' of coloured wool, to link the energy of the person making the namkha with the energy of the five elements; earth, water, fire, air and space.

19 – The Lotus Flower Symbol

It is said that when the baby Prince Siddhartha was born, he immediately walked seven steps and in each footstep a lotus flower appeared from the ground.

It is also said within Vajrayana Buddhism that Padmasambhava (see notes for page 14 and 15) was incarnated as an eight-year-old child and appeared on a lotus blossom which was floating on a lake.

Within Buddhism, the lotus flower symbolises enlightenment. The lotus flower roots lie in dark murky water but from these roots a beautiful flower can grow and rise above the dark and blossom in the light.

20, 21, 22 – Concept of God

Buddhists do not believe in a creator god. They see Buddha Shakyamuni as a human being who achieved enlightenment and perfected the human state. Buddhists do not worship the Buddha but rather contemplate his teachings and his life. Rather than worshipping a divine being, Buddhism centres around the importance of the Buddha's teaching, or the dharma (the right path).

Images of the Buddha form the focus of a shrine at home or in a temple, vihara or centre and offerings of money, fruit, sweets and flowers are often made. As part of the shrine, candles provide a reminder of the Buddha's wisdom, flowers that everything changes and is impermanent and incense as a reminder of the positive effect that good actions have in the wider world.

Some Buddhists chant mantras and may use mala (beads) to help focus the mind on the teachings and their expression of devotion.

Buddhists can reflect upon and show respect for the Buddha's teachings at home where they may have their own shrine and / or at a centre where they may meet with others. There is no set time, place or requirement for Buddhists in this respect. Centres can be anything from a small room in a garden to large residential premises or purpose-built temples. In common, they will have Buddha images which serve to remind followers of their teachings.

Shoes are removed before entering a shrine as a sign of respect and as a practical way of keeping that place clean.

When sitting in a shrine or temple it is respectful not to face feet towards the Buddha images.

22 – Buddhism Around the World
(see also notes for page 14 and 15)

This photograph of Shakyamuni Buddha is taken in Cambodia.

Buddhism is the fourth largest religion with approximately 521 million followers making up about 7% of the worldwide population. It is practised predominantly in Asian countries but with followers also in many other countries across the world. The 2011 census indicates that in the United Kingdom, Buddhists made up about 0.4% of the population.

Since the enlightenment of Shakyamuni Buddha, the Buddha's teachings spread over the centuries to Southeast Asia, and then through Central Asia to China and the rest of East Asia, and finally to Tibet and the further reaches of Central Asia. Often it developed in these regions naturally due to the local interest in the Buddhist beliefs brought to the county by foreign merchants. Sometimes rulers adopted Buddhism to help bring ethics to their people, but no one was forced to convert.

Buddhist teachings can be divided into two broad traditions, with lots of different styles of Buddhism within each tradition:

Theravada ("Way of the Elders") practised largely in Sri Lanka, Myanmar, Thailand, Cambodia and Laos and also now in Pakistan, Afghanistan, eastern and coastal Iran, and Central Asia.

Mahayana ("Greater Vehicle") which is subdivided into several diverse schools, such as Zen, Pure Land and Nichiren, many of which flourish today in East Asia. Mahayana Buddhists believe that there are many Buddhas – those who have become enlightened and known as Buddha.

Mahayana also includes Vajrayana ("Diamond Vehicle") which is predominant in Tibet, Bhutan and Nepal.

Pilgrimage

There is no obligation for Buddhists to make a pilgrimage but there are many places of significance which might be visited such as Buddha's place of birth at Lumbini, enlightenment at Bodh Gaya, first sermon at Deer Park, Sarnath, and his death at Kushinara. There are many sites that are said to house some of the Buddha's relics (remains of his cremated body) and these are also visited such as the Temple of the Sacred Tooth in Kandy, Sri Lanka, Mount Kailash in Tibet or Boudanath in Nepal.

References and useful websites:

www.buddhanet.net
www.arobuddhism.org

Humanism – Wilf

For my family, being humanist means that we try to live a happy life. Looking after ourselves and other people is really important to us. We try to be kind and helpful to make the world a better place for everyone. We look after the planet so that we can enjoy it now and it is safe for the future.

Judaism – Margalit

For my family, being Jewish means that we try to live as G-d wants. We follow G-d's laws that are recorded in the Torah. Making the world a better place by thinking of G-d in everything we do is really important to us. We try to be kind and thoughtful to everyone.

Buddhism – Caitlin

For my family, being a Buddhist means that we try to be kind to everyone and caring towards all living things. We follow the teachings of the Buddhas. We try to think carefully about our actions and our thoughts. We try to be wise and happy.

Christianity – Vesper

For my family, being a Christian means that we try to live as God wants. We follow the teachings of Jesus who lived as God on Earth. Looking after everyone and everything in the world is really important to us. We try to help others and be friends with everyone.

Islam – Yusuf

For my family, being a Muslim means that we try to live as God wants. We follow the teachings of the Qu'ran which were given to the prophet Muhammad(PBUH) by Allah. We try to think of Allah in everything we do. Looking after everyone and everything in the world that Allah created is really important to us.

Sikhism – Krishan

For my family, being a Sikh means that we think about God in all we do and say. We follow the teachings of our Gurus. We work hard and try our best in everything we do. We treat everyone equally and share as much as we can. We try to always be kind and helpful to others.

Hinduism – Nyal

For my family, being a Hindu means that God is really important to us. We follow the teachings of Lord Swaminarayan who lived as God on Earth. Family and friends are important to us. We try to be kind and caring to everyone and everything. We try to give to others as much as we can.

Bahá'í – Nia

For my family, being a Bahá'í means that we try to live as God wants. We follow the teachings of Bahá'u'lláh. We like to be friends with all people from different families, religions and countries. We help our neighbours near and far whenever we can. We try our best to be kind to everyone.

Timeline of Key Figures

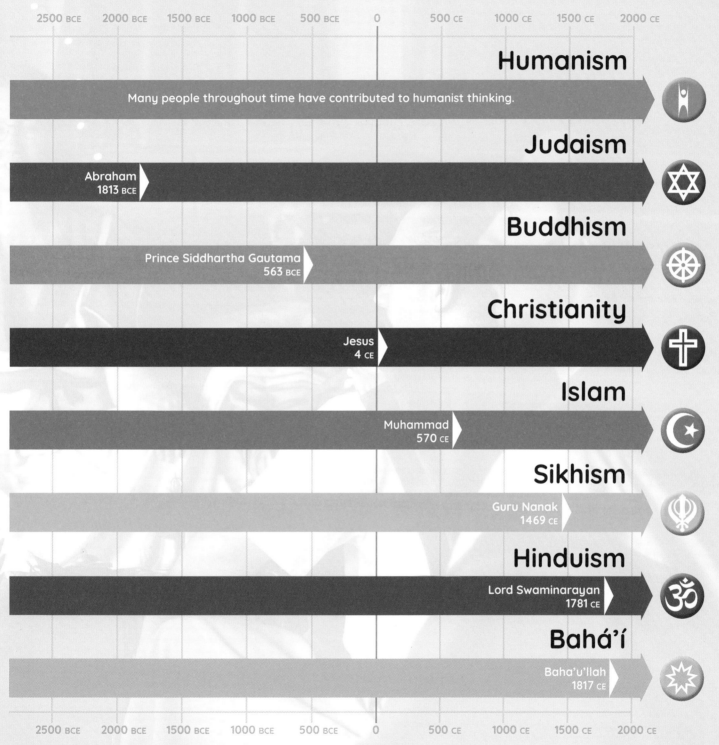

| | 2500 BCE | 2000 BCE | 1500 BCE | 1000 BCE | 500 BCE | 0 | 500 CE | 1000 CE | 1500 CE | 2000 CE |

Humanism
Many people throughout time have contributed to humanist thinking.

Judaism
Abraham 1813 BCE

Buddhism
Prince Siddhartha Gautama 563 BCE

Christianity
Jesus 4 CE

Islam
Muhammad 570 CE

Sikhism
Guru Nanak 1469 CE

Hinduism
Lord Swaminarayan 1781 CE

Bahá'í
Baha'u'llah 1817 CE

| | 2500 BCE | 2000 BCE | 1500 BCE | 1000 BCE | 500 BCE | 0 | 500 CE | 1000 CE | 1500 CE | 2000 CE |

Dates are based on the Gregorian calendar.   BCE = Before Common Era   CE = Common Era

Some key figure birth dates are approximate or may vary according to the source of information. Key figures referenced do not necessarily denote the beginning of the religion / belief system but are those with a particular focus in this series of books. There are, of course, many other significant figures within and across these religions and worldviews. This timeline should be considered alongside the teachers'/ parents'/ carers' notes of each book, to understand the historical context and possible origin of beliefs, as appropriate.

Books at Press

Published by
Books at Press
7 Butlers Mead, Millend, Blakeney,
Gloucestershire GL15 4EH

ISBN: 978-1-8380021-1-4
First published in the UK 2021

Text © Gill Vaisey 2021
Illustrations © Janette Louden 2021
Photography © Joanna Nicholls 2021

The rights of Gill Vaisey, Janette Louden
and Joanna Nicholls to be identified as
the author, illustrator and photographer
of this work has been asserted by them in
accordance with the Copyright, Designs
and Patents Act 1988.

Design by David Rose
Printed by ADverts, Latvia

Acknowledgements:
Many thanks are extended to the family
members and wider community involved
in the creation of this book and its
accompanying resources.

Particular thanks are extended to Ngakma
Shé-zér Khandro and Ngakpa Namgyal
Dorje for their invaluable contribution to
the main text and the teachers' / parents' /
carers' notes.

Thanks also to Martin Holmes for his
continued support and editing.

I am indebted to Joanna Nicholls who
has shared this amazing journey with
me and has been much more than chief
photographer!

Celebrating Diversity

In reading this book and its accompanying notes, it must be recognised that, as with many other religions and belief systems, there is diversity among communities, families and individuals in the way in which the faith is observed and expressed. This can be influenced by the particular tradition followed, personal choice and local culture. This book reflects one family's expression of their faith. It should not be portrayed as the only expression of Buddhism. Diversity of beliefs and practices should always be acknowledged.

Also available in the **Belonging and Believing** series:

Belonging and Believing: My Hindu Family — Gill Vaisey
Belonging and Believing: My Bahá'í Family — Gill Vaisey
Belonging and Believing: My Sikh Family — Gill Vaisey
Belonging and Believing: My Muslim Family — Gill Vaisey
Belonging and Believing: My Christian Family — Gill Vaisey
Belonging and Believing: My Jewish Family — Gill Vaisey
Belonging and Believing: My Humanist Family — Gill Vaisey

www.booksatpress.co.uk